# Contents

## 1 First put on the underclothes.

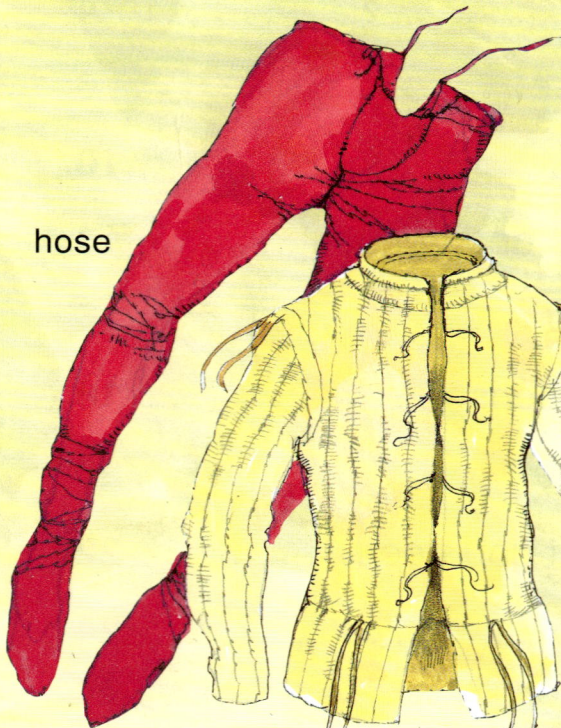

hose

doublet

knight

squire

3

## ◆2 Next cover his feet.

sabatons

# 3 Then cover his legs.

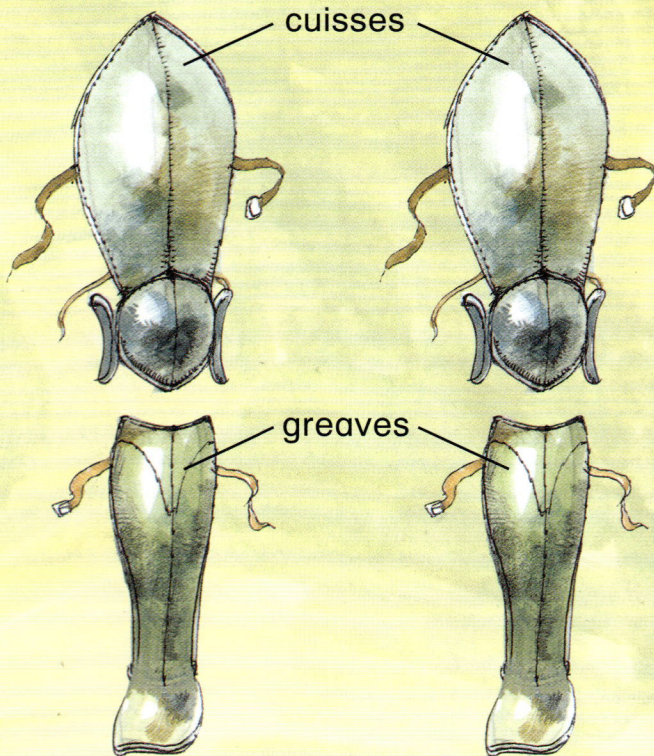

cuisses

greaves

# 4 ◆ Put the mail skirt on.

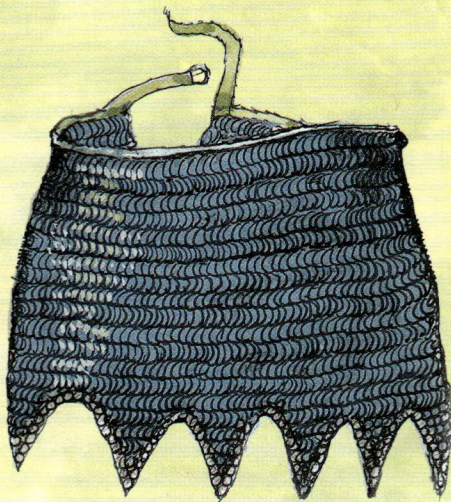

mail skirt

**5** **Now put on the backplate ...**

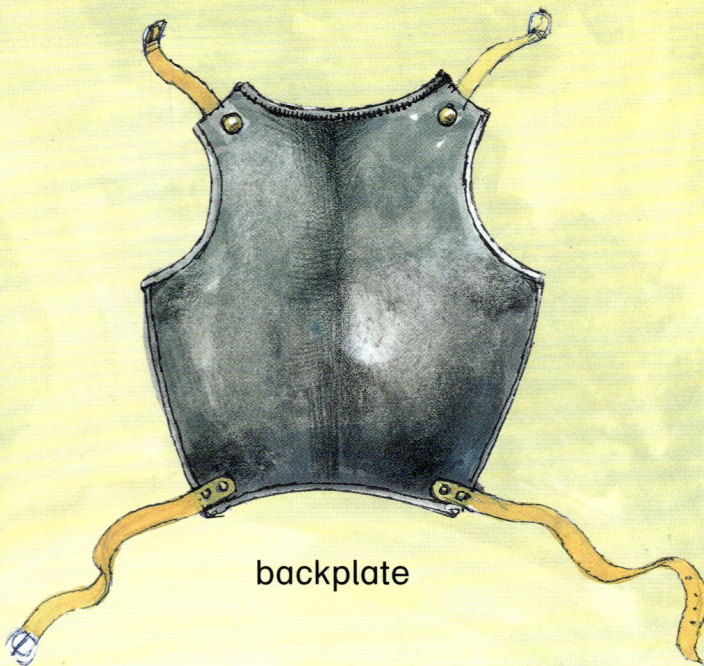

backplate

# ... and the breastplate.

breastplate

## 6 Cover his arms and hands.

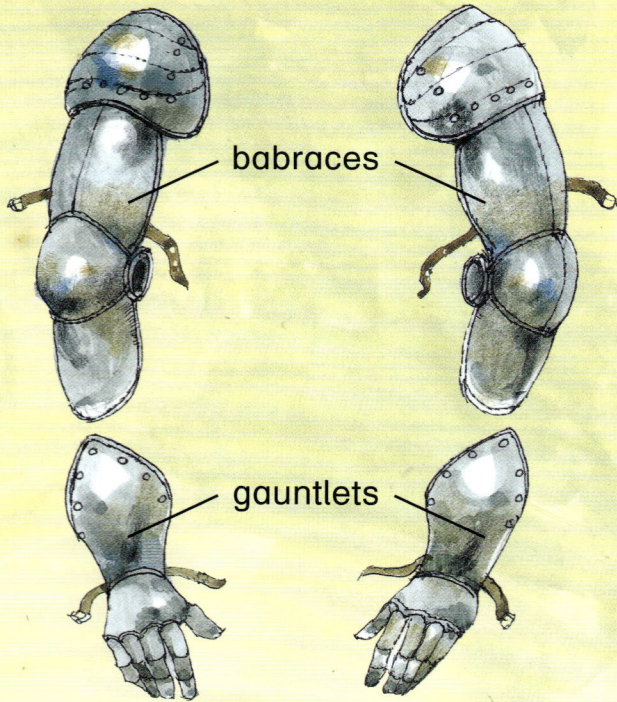

babraces

gauntlets

**7** **Then put the helmet on his head.**

helmet

## 8 ◆ Give him his sword.

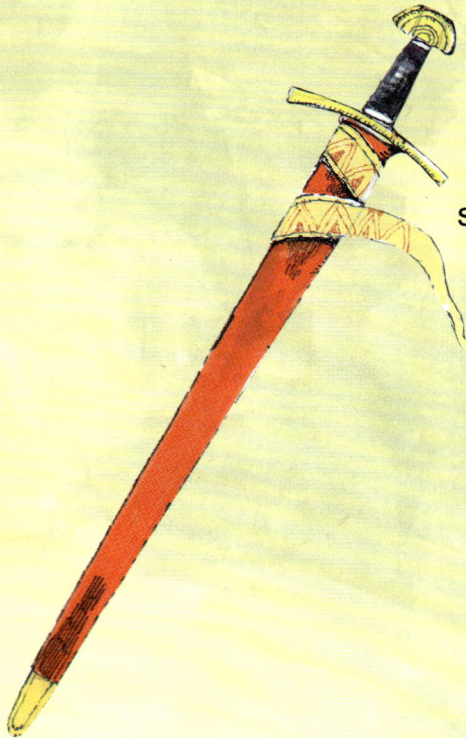

sword

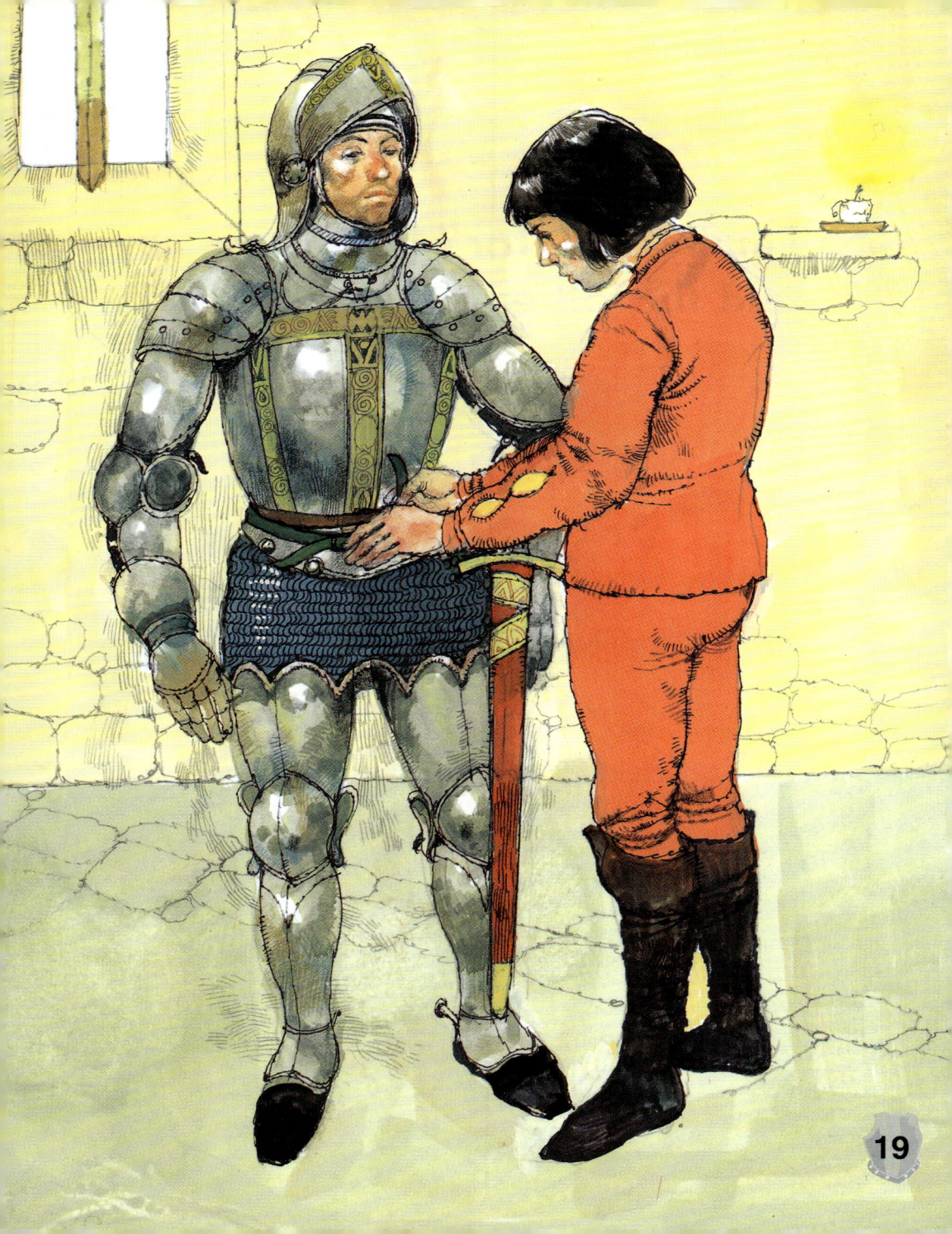

**9** Finally, call for his horse and the other squires.

lance

shield

When the knight is on his horse, he is given the shield and lance.

# What you need

helmet

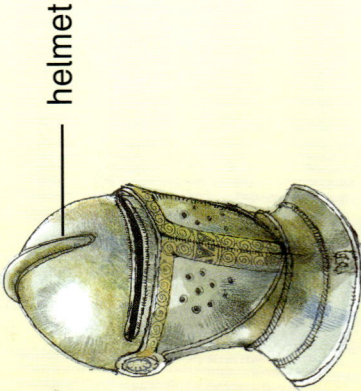

breastplate

backplate

babraces

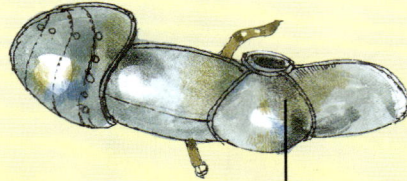

gauntlets

lance

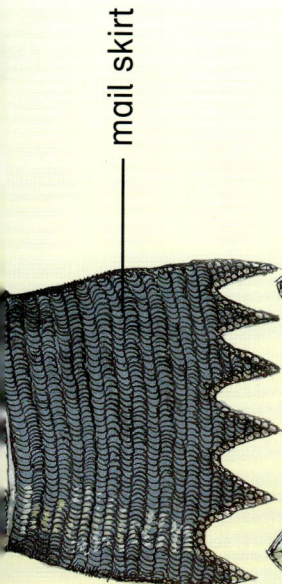

mail skirt

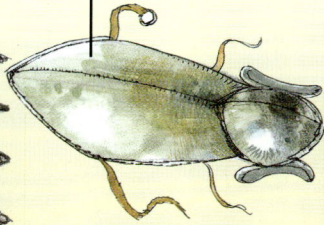

cuisses

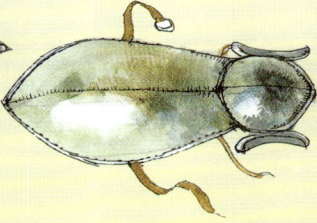

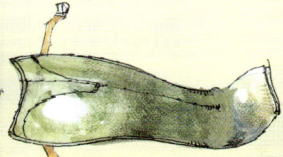

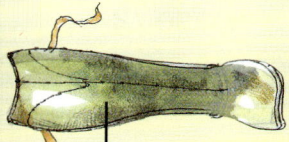

greaves

sabatons

sword

# Index